D0688122

Leonardo da Vinci

Artist, Inventor, and Renaissance Man

MAKERS OF THE MIDDLE AGES AND RENAISSANCE

Leonardo da Vinci

Artist, Inventor, and Renaissance Man

Rachel A. Koestler-Grack

CHELSEA HOUSE
PUBLISHERS
A Haights Cross Communications ⌁ Company ®
Philadelphia

COVER: Anonymous portrait of Leonardo da Vinci. Uffizi, Florence, Italy.

CHELSEA HOUSE PUBLISHERS
VP, NEW PRODUCT DEVELOPMENT Sally Cheney
DIRECTOR OF PRODUCTION Kim Shinners
CREATIVE MANAGER Takeshi Takahashi
MANUFACTURING MANAGER Diann Grasse

Staff for Leonardo da Vinci
EXECUTIVE EDITOR Lee Marcott
EDITORIAL ASSISTANT Carla Greenberg
PRODUCTION EDITOR Noelle Nardone
COVER AND INTERIOR DESIGNER Keith Trego
LAYOUT 21st Century Publishing and Communications, Inc.

A Haights Cross Communications ↙ Company ®

www.chelseahouse.com

First Printing

9 8 7 6 5 4 3 2 1

Library of Congress Cataloging-in-Publication Data

Koestler-Grack, Rachel A., 1973–
    Leonardo da Vinci: artist, inventor, and Renaissance man/Rachel Koestler-Grack.
      p. cm.–(Makers of the Middle Ages and Renaissance)
    Includes bibliographical references and index.
    ISBN 0-7910-8626-7 (hard cover)
1. Leonardo, da Vinci, 1452–1519—Juvenile literature. 2. Artists—Italy—
Biography—Juvenile literature. 3. Inventors—Italy—Biography—Juvenile literature.
I. Title. II. Series.
N6923.L33K645 2005
709'.2–dc22
                                                              2005007490

CONTENTS

Renaissance Man

As Leonardo da Vinci walked into the damp dining room of the Convent of Santa Marie delle Grazie, he could smell a trace of linseed oil in the air. A half-painted mural covered one of the walls. He stood about ten feet back from the wall and gazed at his work. For a long time, he studied the images. He shuffled to the

1

other side of the room and, again, stood staring for several minutes. He then paced to the opposite side of the room and continued the process of reviewing his work.

Finally he shook his head in disapproval and leaned in close to the painting. Raising one corner of his mouth in a smile, he nodded. He quickly picked up his brush and began retouching his previous day's work. Perhaps the shading was not quite right. Maybe the folds in a cloak did not show the outline of an arm. He liked his work to shine with magnificence. If something were not quite right, he would change it.

On this day, Leonardo da Vinci was working on his famous mural—*The Last Supper*. He would labor with brush strokes and colors from dawn until dark. Then, for three or four days, he would not step foot in the convent. This was how he worked. Although his methods frustrated his employers, few dared to argue with the master.

Leonardo da Vinci was born in 1452, in the middle of the Italian Renaissance—a time of great discovery and rebirth in the arts, literature, and the sciences. Because the Italian peninsula juts out into

Leonardo da Vinci's most famous mural was *The Last Supper*. This detail of that mural shows the apostles to the far left of the painting.

the Mediterranean Sea, the sea had long been the main trading route between Europe and the East Indies. Trade with distant lands brought with it new ideas. During the Renaissance, Italy became the center of fresh thoughts, while Italian artists set new trends in painting, architecture, and sculpture. Many artists and scholars traveled to Italy to study and learn.

The Renaissance marked a rebirth in many subject areas. Europeans took a new interest in ancient Greek scholars, writers, and teachers, while a fresh study of religion helped start the Protestant Reformation, led by Martin Luther and others who questioned the teachings of the Catholic Church.

As artists began painting more realistic scenes, they discovered that they could create depth by painting faraway objects smaller. In order to do this, they drew diagonal lines into the picture. Next they painted objects in the background increasingly smaller as they got further away. Artists also used light and shading to give their paintings texture and shine. They could make a velvet cloak shimmer in a painting just as it did in life.

The Renaissance was also a time of European exploration and discoveries about the world. Explorers found sea routes to Asia and new lands in the West, including North America and the Caribbean. Inventors discovered how to create new navigational instruments, such as the compass. Leonardo da Vinci was a true Renaissance man. He had many talents and accomplishments. He was gifted in so many areas, it was difficult for him to choose which talents to pursue and master. He finally abandoned the idea of making a choice and threw himself into learning everything. Leonardo da Vinci was driven to learn all of the sciences and all of the arts, and to explore the workings of machinery. He was a painter, a sculptor, an inventor, an engineer, a writer, an architect, and even some-thing of a scientist.

Test Your Knowledge

1 The Mediterranean Sea had long been a
trade route between which two areas of
the world?
a. Asia and Africa
b. Europe and the East Indies
c. Europe and Asia
d. Europe and the West Indies

2 Who led the Protestant Reformation?
a. Martin Luther
b. Pope Leo X
c. Leonardo da Vinci
d. John the Baptist

3 What technique did Renaissance artists use to
create depth?
a. Painting faraway objects larger
b. Painting objects close up larger
c. Painting faraway objects smaller
d. Painting with muted background colors

4 Which navigational instrument was invented
during the Renaissance?
a. The telescope
b. The map
c. A ship's sextant
d. The compass

5 In addition to art, in which area(s) did Leonardo da Vinci show talent?

a. As an engineer

b. As an inventor

c. As a scientist

d. All of the above

ANSWERS: 1. b; 2. a; 3. c; 4. d; 5. d

A Lonely Genius

The landscape around Florence, Italy, has not changed much in the last 500 years. Clusters of red-roofed houses, seemingly tossed like dice, sit across the low hills. Terraced vineyards hug small towns, and the silvery leaves of olive trees glitter in the breeze. Off in the distance, red and white poppies mix with the long,

8

This simple stone house, in the Tuscan town of Vinci, was the birthplace of Leonardo da Vinci. It was a home befitting the humble beginnings of one of the world's greatest artists.

mountain grass, below the steep slopes of Monte Albano. Here, in the small Tuscan town of Vinci, Leonardo da Vinci was born, on April 15, 1452.

The birth of a child to a peasant woman was not usually an event welcomed with grand celebration. Leonardo's birth was a humble occurrence, probably taking place in a small, simple stone house, but Leonardo's grandfather Antonio was proud enough of the baby's arrival to note it in his journal. He wrote: "1452: there was a born to me a grandson, the child of Ser Piero my son."[1]

Leonardo's father, Piero da Vinci, came from a respected family, which was neither noble nor wealthy, but had a good reputation in the surrounding towns. Leonardo's grandfather, Antonio, and his grandmother, Monna, owned a farm outside of Vinci, where they tended olive groves and worked fields of wheat and buckwheat. They had three children— Piero, who was 25 years old when Leonardo was born; daughter Violante; and a 16-year-old son named Francesco.

Leonardo's father was not married to his mother, Caterina. The couple stayed together for some time, but they never married. As a promising young lawyer, Piero da Vinci probably wanted to marry a noble woman—someone whose parents could provide a dowry. This marriage gift of property or money would help Piero da Vinci establish a business in the nearby city of Florence. Caterina's family was poor and could not provide a dowry.

Nonetheless, Piero da Vinci was probably drawn to Caterina's beauty. Leonardo later sketched a picture of his mother, a woman of lovely, delicate features. "Have you not seen peasant girls in the mountains," Leonardo wrote, "clad in their poor rags, bereft [deprived of] all ornaments, yet surpassing in beauty women covered with ornaments?"[2] Leonardo's comment was no doubt referring to the remarkable beauty of his mother. However, while Piero da Vinci and Caterina may have been in love, she obviously did not fit into his plans for a prestigious career and marriage.

Soon after Leonardo was born, his mother married a local man whose nickname was Accattabriga—"the Mischiefmaker." Leonardo da Vinci's mother also gave birth to a daughter, Piera, in 1454, when Leonardo was two years old. Three more children quickly followed—Lisabetta, Francesco, and Sandra. Leonardo was jealous of his half sisters and half brother. He did not like sharing his mother's attention. He felt that his half sisters and half brother were more special because they lived with both of their parents, in the same house.

Leonardo's home life soon changed. When he was about five years old, he went to live with his grandfather, Antonio. By this time, his father had

Piero da Vinci was drawn to Caterina, the beautiful woman who would become Leonardo da Vinci's mother. Leonardo later sketched *Head of a Woman* (shown here) as a tribute to his mother's beauty.

married Albiera di Giovanni Amadori, from a fine Florentine family. Piero Da Vinci and his new wife lived in Florence, a day's journey away from Vinci, but Leonardo's father made the trip as often as he could.

Leonardo had a troubled childhood. He rarely saw his mother and father, instead spending most of his time with his grandfather. Leonardo must have felt lost, like he did not belong anywhere. The closest thing to a father figure he had was probably his Uncle Francesco. When his uncle finally got married, Leonardo must have felt betrayed.

Leonardo was a country boy. As a child, he learned how to plough, plant, and harvest. He undoubtedly worked in the orchards, grain fields, vineyards, and olive groves around his grandfather's farm. In those days, as is still true today, olives played an important part in everyday life. Olive oil was used in cooking, to fuel lamps, for medicine, and as an ointment for cuts, scrapes, and rashes. Leonardo loved the outdoors and spent hours wandering the flowering meadows, climbing the rocky hillside, and relaxing under the shade of the chestnut trees.

One day, while young Leonardo took a break from hiking in the mountains, he noticed a layer of rock high up in a cave. Shells and bones had become embedded in the stone. Leonardo recognized them as being some sort of sea creature. The shells appeared to have turned into stone, or fossils, as we call them today. At that time, Leonardo did not know about fossils. He wondered how the shells had gotten to the cave, miles away from the sea and hundreds of feet above the water.

Despite his abundant curiosity and sharp mind, Leonardo did not like school. He often neglected his reading and mathematics lessons. He preferred to learn in his own way, by observing the world around him. He tried to find answers to things that puzzled him. One of the most unusual and fascinating things about young Leonardo was his "mirror writing." Throughout his life, he worried about the possibility of others stealing his ideas. The observations in his notebooks were written in such a way that they could only be read by holding the books up to a mirror. He wrote his notes backwards, from right to left, and he also formed each letter in reverse. For example, a Leonardo *d* looked like a

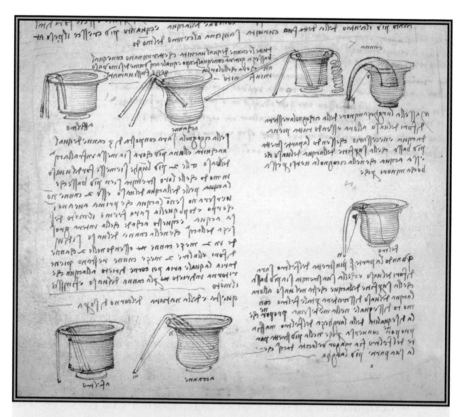

A page of Leonardo da Vinci's "mirror writing, " the technique he invented to take notes about his observations, is shown here. The observations in his notebooks were written in such a way that they could only be read by holding the books up to a mirror.

normal *b*. This talent, no doubt, took an exceptional mind. From a very early age, Leonardo da Vinci showed signs of genius.

As he journeyed through the countryside, young Leonardo always carried a notebook. If something

Leonardo's Notebooks

Much of what we know about Leonardo da Vinci comes from his notebooks. After his death, his favorite pupil, Francesco Melzi, inherited almost all of his writings. Today Leonardo da Vinci's manuscripts are divided into ten different books.

The "Codex Arundel" is a collection of Leonardo da Vinci's work that deals with a variety of subjects. The 283 pages of text include notes on geometry, weights, and architecture. Leonardo da Vinci wrote these notes between 1480 and 1518. Today the collection is kept in the British Library in London.

The "Codex Atlanticus" is a huge book of Leonardo da Vinci's drawings, from 1480 to 1518. The volume is called "Codex Atlanticus" because of its "ocean" size. The drawings include astronomy, botany, zoology, and military arts. It is held by the Biblioteca Ambrosiana in Milan.

Between 1487 and 1490, Leonardo da Vinci kept notes on his studies of architecture and religion. These writings are in the "Codex Trivulzianus." The Codex "On the Flight of Birds" includes Leonardo da Vinci's observations on how birds take off, land, and move in the air.

The "Codex Ashburnham" and "Codices of the Institut de France" are kept in the Institute de France, in Paris. The Ashburnham notebook consists of two cardboard-bound manuscripts, which contain pictures and drawings, probably sketched from 1489 to 1492. The codices include many notes and pictures on various subjects, including optics and hydraulics.

The "Codex Forster" and "Codex Leicester" contain more notes from Leonardo da Vinci's studies, from different time periods. The "Codex Leicester" is the only manuscript in private hands. Bill Gates purchased the writings in 1995.

The "Windsor folios," a 600-page drawing book, contains drawings of various sizes in subjects such as anatomy, geography, horses, and maps. Leonardo da Vinci sketched these pictures between 1478 and 1518.

Finally, the "Madrid Codices" were discovered in 1966. They consist of two manuscripts—"Madrid I" and "Madrid II"—and are bound in red morocco, a type of leather. These notebooks contain mostly writings and drawings in mechanics.

captured his attention, he quickly pulled out a notebook and made a sketch. Leonardo especially enjoyed animals. He drew pictures of birds, lizards, cats, dogs, horses, oxen, bears, and lions. All living creatures fascinated him, and he studied their every movement. Next to one of his early drawings, he wrote, "If at night you place your eye between the light and the eye of a cat, you will see that its eye seems to be on fire."[3]

Before long, it became obvious that Leonardo had an incredible talent for drawing. In fifteenth-century Italy, drawing, painting, and sculpting were not just hobbies. Because there were no cameras or photographs, painting was the only way to create images of famous people and important events in history.

Piero da Vinci was aware of his son's talent, so he arranged for young Leonardo to become an apprentice of a well-known artist named Andrea del Verrocchio. At about the age of ten, Leonardo prepared to make another move. This time, he was on his way to Florence, to study under the watchful eye of a great painter and sculptor.

Test Your Knowledge

1 How did Leonardo da Vinci's grandparents
   earn a living?
   a. As farmers
   b. As winemakers
   c. As bankers
   d. As merchants

2 How old was Leonardo da Vinci's father when
   Leonardo was born?
   a. 22
   b. 17
   c. 25
   d. 29

3 What was a dowry?
   a. A marriage gift of food
   b. A marriage gift of property or money
   c. A marriage gift of art
   d. All of the above

4 About how old was Leonardo da Vinci when
   he went to live with his grandfather?
   a. Three
   b. Ten
   c. Seven
   d. Five

5 What did young Leonardo find while hiking
one day?

a. A fossil

b. An ancient artifact

c. A precious stone

d. A secret cave

ANSWERS: 1. a; 2. c; 3. b; 4. d; 5. a

The Young Apprentice

When Leonardo was young, Florence was one of the most prosperous and lively cities in Italy. It was a hub for trade and a huge exporter of cloth. All sorts of fabrics were manufactured in Florence—including silk, velvet, brightly colored wools, and shiny brocades of gold and silver. The city was also famous for its goldsmiths, who fastened jewels onto plates and other gold objects.

Leonardo must have been amazed by the busy city streets of Florence. Bustling city life was very different from the quiet countryside of Vinci. The young artist must have been nervous as he walked into Verrocchio's studio, or *bottega*. As he passed through the door, he noticed a beautiful landscape painting in the window. Inside, the work benches were cluttered with knives and chisels for sculpting, and sketches and plans. Easels held blank wooden pieces ready to be painted, and half-shaped sculptures stood on turntables.

Leonardo closed his eyes and took a deep breath. He let the smell of paints, wood, and clay fill his lungs. For the first time, he felt like a real artist. He was excited to learn from his new teacher. Leonardo was not the only student at the studio. Some of his classmates—such as Sandro Botticelli, Pietro Vanucci, and Lorenzo di Credi—would also go on to become well-known artists. The studio was similar to a university; the art students could have discussions about ideas and techniques.

After Leonardo had been studying for a while, his father provided him with an opportunity to

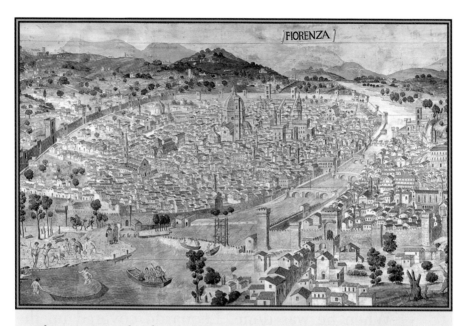

When Leonardo da Vinci was young, Florence, Italy, (shown here in 1480) was one of the most vibrant, lively cities in Italy. Florence was a center for trade, and fabrics, such as silk and velvet, were made there.

demonstrate what he had learned. A peasant came to Piero da Vinci's home carrying a large round piece of wood from a fig tree. He thought it would make a nice shield. Shields were painted, round plaques that people hung outside the door of their home.

The peasant approached Leonardo's father and asked if perhaps he knew of someone who could paint the shield for a fair price. Piero da Vinci promised to find someone, and he brought the piece of wood to 13-year-old Leonardo, encouraging his son to try to make something out of it.[4]

Eager to impress his father, Leonardo went out into the wilderness. He captured and killed small animals and insects to be the subjects of his painting. As he worked, he was surrounded by lizards, snakes, bats, dragonflies, and crickets. He painted a different feature from each animal—the eyes of one creature and the jaw from another, for example. From all of them, he created a fire-breathing dragon.

When he was done, Leonardo covered up the window, leaving only a single beam of light to fall on the shield. Eager to unveil his masterpiece, Leonardo called to his father. Piero da Vinci was not accustomed to such realistic artwork. For a moment, he thought the dragon was real, and he turned away. Leonardo beamed with pride in the knowledge that his work could create such a strong emotion.

Piero da Vinci knew the work was valuable. Instead of selling it to the peasant, he bought another shield—one with a simple heart and arrow painted on it. He gave the simple shield to the peasant, who cherished it for the rest of his life. Piero da Vinci then sold Leonardo's shield to a wealthy man, for a

As a young boy, eager to impress his father, Leonardo da Vinci combined features from many different animals to create a painting of a fire-breathing dragon. This image, *Fight Between a Dragon and a Lion*, illustrates Leonardo da Vinci's skill at painting animals.

good price. Eventually, it is believed, the shield was bought by the Duke of Milan for three times the amount that Piero da Vinci had originally sold it for.

Around this time, Piero's da Vinci's wife, Albiera, died. After 12 years of being unable to have children, she died during the birth of her first child. She was buried in June 1464. Piero da Vinci quickly remarried a 17-year-old woman named Francesca. She died 11 years later, and Piero da Vinci married again, this time to a woman named Margnerita. At the time, Piero da Vinci was 47 years old and Margnerita was just 17. Over ten years, the couple had four sons and two daughters. When Margnerita died, Piero da Vinci took a fouth bride—Lucrezia. In seven years of marriage, Lucrezia had one daughter and five sons. The last son was born when Piero da Vinci was in his 70s.

LEARNING THE ART

Leonardo da Vinci started his training with drafts-manship, or *disengo*. Drafting was the foundation of every artist's education. Students who were younger than 20 were not allowed to touch brushes or colors. Instead they practiced with a lead stylus. Before moving on to shading and color, teachers thought it was important for all students to master the use of simple lines. Leonardo da Vinci was painting before he was 20, but he also began by learning to draft. He used this same approach when he later became a teacher.

During his apprenticeship, Leonardo da Vinci imitated Verrocchio's work, which was exactly what a student of that time was supposed to do, but he was bothered by this limitation in his creativity. Leonardo da Vinci believed that a student could never reach his full potential without creating his own work. He did not strive to be like Verrocchio. He desired to be better. "The pupil who does not outstrip his master is mediocre," he wrote.[5]

In many ways, Leonardo da Vinci did exceed his master. He was a brilliant artist of draperies. He first made a clay model. Then he dipped rags in plaster and draped them over the figure. He would carefully draw the image with the point of his brush, trying to capture every fold, pleat, and flow of the fabric. He showed remarkable talent in his draperies. He took them beyond simple exercises, turning them into true art forms. He later wrote that a drapery "must fit the body and not appear like an empty bundle of clothes."[6]

Another part of Leonardo da Vinci's apprenticeship involved modeling in clay and terracotta. An artist who lived during the same time as Leonardo wrote, "In his youth, [Leonardo] made in clay

As a boy, Leonardo da Vinci was a talented young student. He was a brilliant artist of draperies. Leonardo da Vinci later completed this seated figure, *Drapery Study on Linen.*

several heads of laughing women . . . as well as some children's heads."[7] As far as anyone knows, however, none of his models survived into the present day. Because of the lack of works from his early years, Leonardo da Vinci's early career as a sculptor remains somewhat of a mystery. One particular terracotta head called *Youthful Christ* is believed by some to be his work, but experts disagree. One possible owner wrote:

> I have also a little terracotta head of Christ when he was a boy, sculpted by Leonardo Vinci's own hand, in which one sees the simplicity and purity of the boy, together with a certain something which shows wisdom, intellect and majesty.[8]

Leonardo da Vinci clearly had a gift for bringing his sculptures to life. By carefully molding their expressions, he was able to create figures with lifelike personalities.

Leonardo da Vinci also learned the techniques of molding and carving in relief, art forms created by carving raised images into a flat surface. At the Louvre Museum in Paris, France, a pair of terracotta angels in relief is on display. The angels came from the Verrocchio studio. Many people believe Leonardo da Vinci helped to carve the pieces. The angels are strikingly similar to the painted angel in his *Baptism of Christ*.

After Leonardo da Vinci mastered drafting and clay modeling, he moved on to painting. In those days, paper was expensive and canvas was not yet in use, so artists painted on wood panels. Long before Leonardo da Vinci ever put a paintbrush to a panel, however, he learned how to prepare his painting surface. He studied different types of wood, such as poplar, walnut, and pear. White poplar was the type of wood used by most studios. This wood was inexpensive and easy to use. Regardless of the wood used, the panels had to be properly oiled and primed before painting could begin. The final layers of gypsum-based white "primer" formed a silky, smooth, bright white surface. The primer would not absorb the paint, helping to keep the colors vibrant and true.

Leonardo da Vinci also made his own paints. His colors came from plants, barks, earth, and minerals. He ground the collected items into a powdered pigment. When he first began painting, he used tempera paints. Tempera is any kind of binding substance that will "temper," or blend, powdered colors and make them workable as paint. For Leonardo da Vinci, the tempera was egg. He mixed the colors with fresh egg yolk and thinned the mixture with water. Egg tempera dried almost immediately, a few shades lighter than when it was wet. Paint, wood, and clay were not the only smells at the *bottega*, and the clanking of tools was not the only sound. Verrocchio certainly would have raised his own chickens for eggs, and the clucks of hens would have added to the noise level.

Eventually artists began using oil-based paints. These paints took longer to dry, but kept their vibrant colors. Painters used different types of oils in their pigments, but the most common was linseed oil. Sometimes they also used walnut oil. Leonardo da Vinci experimented with different plants and oils. He added turpentine and crushed mustard seed to his colors. He was constantly trying to improve his materials and the quality of his work.

After the paints were prepared, the picture could be transferred onto the panel. Most paintings started as a black and white drawing on paper. Leonardo da Vinci carefully pricked tiny holes in the surface of the paper, outlining each image. These perforations can be seen on many of his drawings. He then fixed the drawing flat against the panel and dusted the

A Bitter Enemy

Leonardo da Vinci was not the only great artist of the Renaissance. Other artists of the Italian Renaissance included Giotto, Donatello, and Brunelleschi. Leonardo da Vinci, however, developed an especially intense dislike for a rising young artist named Michelangelo.

Michelangelo was born on March 6, 1475, in Caprese, Tuscany, but he always considered himself a native of Florence. When he was 13 years old, Michelangelo became an apprentice in the workshop of painter Domenico Ghirlandaio. After one year of painting frescos, he went on to study sculpture in the Medici gardens in Florence. About this time, he probably first met Leonardo da Vinci. Michelangelo quickly became a favorite of Lorenzo de' Medici's, which may have intensified Leonardo da Vinci's feelings of jealousy.

Like Leonardo da Vinci, Michelangelo also studied anatomy. He used his knowledge of the human body to create lifelike sculptures. One of his most famous sculptures was of the biblical hero David. The statue stands over 14 feet tall. Leonardo da Vinci later sketched a similar David drawing in his notebooks.

While Leonardo da Vinci was painting his mural of the Battle of Anghiari, Michelangelo began a cartoon of another fresco that would be painted on the opposite wall. Michelangelo was to paint a fresco of another Florentine victory—the Battle of Cascina. This new painting sparked some competition between the two artists. They wanted to see who could outdo the other in creative genius. The friendly competition quickly turned into a bitter rivalry.

After Leonardo da Vinci saw Michelangelo's cartoon of the battle, he made a comment in one of his notebooks. "You should not make all the muscles of the body too conspicuous," he wrote, "unless the limbs to which they belong are engaged in the exertion of great force or labor." He added, "Otherwise you will produce a sack of walnuts rather than a human figure."* His comment may have been a dig on Michelangelo's drawings.

Just like Leonardo da Vinci, Michelangelo never finished his mural. He was called away to Rome where he began painting the now-famous Sistine Chapel ceiling in the Vatican. Both men being giants in the world of art, it is difficult to say who would have "won" the mural competition.

* Charles Nicoll, *Leonardo da Vinci: Flights of the Mind.* New York: Penguin Group, 2004. p. 382.

paper with finely powdered charcoal or pumice. This process was known as pouncing. During pouncing, the dust settled through the holes of the drawing, leaving an outline of the picture on the panel, ready for painting.

Finally Leonardo da Vinci was ready to paint. In practice, this task meant painting only a part of the artwork, as Renaissance workshops were a collaborative effort. A work created by a certain artist was often only partially painted by him. The rest of the image was often painted by the assistants and apprentices under him.

One example of a combined painting from Verrocchio's studio is a small panel painting of *Tobias and the Angel.* The piece was painted between 1468 and 1470. The story of Tobias told of a young boy's quest to heal his father's blindness. During his adventure, Tobias was under the guardianship of the angel Raphael. The story was much like a fairy tale. Verrocchio's painting included a fish and a dog. Verrocchio was not skilled at painting animals, but Leonardo da Vinci was. In the artwork, a terrier trots alongside the angel. The dog looks alive and alert. Its long silky fur looks much like the hair of

Leonardo da Vinci's angels. Likewise, the fish scales shimmer and reflect the light, a detail Verrocchio probably would not have captured. Most likely, Leonardo da Vinci added these touches to the painting. All of the elements he contributed—a lively dog, a glistening fish, Tobias's curly hair— would become the trademarks of this gifted apprentice in the years to come.

Test Your Knowledge

1   When Leonardo da Vinci was young, Florence was know as an exporter of
   a. marble.
   b. silver.
   c. gold.
   d. cloth.

2   One of Leonardo da Vinci's classmates in Verrocchio's studio was
   a. Sandro Botticelli.
   b. Michelangelo.
   c. Claude Monet.
   d. Pablo Picasso.

3   What type of animal did young Leonardo paint on the shield his father gave him?
   a. A lizard
   b. An eagle
   c. A fire-breathing dragon
   d. A knight's horse

4   How old was Piero da Vinci when his last son was born?
   a. In his 60s
   b. In his 70s
   c. In his 40s
   d. In his 50s

5 What type of wood was used by most art studios?
a. Oak
b. Pear
c. Walnut
d. White poplar

ANSWERS: 1. d; 2. a; 3. c; 4. b; 5. d

First
Paintings

On February 7, 1469, a jousting match was held in
Florence to honor 20-year-old Lorenzo de' Medici.
The Medicis were bankers who had made a tremendous
fortune. They gained power in Florence by lending great
amounts of money to people outside the city walls. Their
borrowers included kings, dukes, and even popes.

38

In the 1400s, Italy was not yet a unified nation. Instead the country was divided into many small city-states. The people did not call themselves Italians. Instead they named themselves after the area in which they lived. They were Venetians, Romans, Milanese, or Tuscans. Although the members of the Medici family did not yet have any actual political power in Italy, their wealth and influence made them more like lords than businessmen.

The February celebration welcomed Lorenzo de' Medici into public life and celebrated his upcoming marriage to Clarice Orsini. As he rode his horse through the city streets in a grand parade, colorful banners of silk, taffeta, and velvet fluttered above him. The sunlight bouncing off his armor looked like shooting stars. At his side, he carried a long white charger, a gift from the king of Naples.

In those days, jousts and carnivals were popular public events. For this event, Verrocchio's workshop had created all of the artwork on the costumes, masks, armor, decorative wagons, and banners. Verrocchio also designed Lorenzo de' Medici's coat of arms, which was displayed on his banner.

Sacred shows that took place on holy days were another form of public theater. These performances were big productions with great special effects. Huge revolving disks were used to change the scenery. Wires and pulleys helped the actors fly through the air. Leonardo da Vinci watched the shows in wonder. He, no doubt, saw the performance of the Annunciation—a story about the angel Gabriel descending from heaven to the Virgin Mary. During this visit, the angel tells Mary how she will give birth to the Christ child.

Leonardo da Vinci was dazzled by the energy and splendor of the theater. As the handsome, young artist stood at the edge of the crowd admiring the entertainment, he had a quizzical look on his face at all times. He was not just watching the events. He was studying how everything was done.

HIS OWN PAINTINGS

In the summer of 1472, Leonardo da Vinci joined Compagnia di San Luca—a fraternity of Florentine painters. Founded in the mid-1300s, the "artists club" was made up of a loose group of painters of all kinds. Other branches of the fraternity met in Siena

A detail from Leonardo da Vinci's *Annunciation* is shown here. While many Renaissance artists depicted this popular subject, Leonardo da Vinci's *Annunciation* dramatized the moment when Mary was visited by the angel Gabriel.

and Milan. Later, fraternities also began in Rome, Paris, and London.

During this time, Leonardo da Vinci finished his painting called *The Annunciation*. He certainly would have used the sacred theater shows as inspiration for this work. The subject matter was the most popular theme in Renaissance art. Almost every important painter made at least one version of it. Leonardo's *Annunciation* dramatized the moment when Mary was visited by the angel Gabriel, when she was told she would become the mother of the Messiah.

Most artists of the time tried to express the whole range of emotions in their Anunciation paintings. In Leonardo da Vinci's painting, Mary was clearly troubled by Gabriel's news. She thought deeply about it, questioned her worthiness, and finally submitted to the decision. In Leonardo da Vinci's painting, not all emotions were present. The painting seemed to have a before and after, as though the image were caught at just one moment in time. Leonardo da Vinci also portrayed Mary reading the Bible at the time. The angel caught her unexpectedly as she was reading the Old Testament prophesies of the coming Christ child.

At about this same time, Leonardo da Vinci finished another painting of Mary, this one with the baby Jesus. The *Madonna of the Carnation* looks much like the Virgin Mary in *The Annunciation.* They both wear the same blue dress with red sleeves. Mary also wears a glittering topaz pin, an image that later became Leonardo da Vinci's signature in his

Farmland around Vinci, Italy, is shown here. Landscapes resembling the Tuscan countryside near Vinci were included in some of da Vinci's paintings.

painting. The landscape in the background suggests, even more, that this painting was Leonardo da Vinci's work. A rocky mountain range rises in the distance, and the rolling hills resemble the Tuscan view near Vinci.

Another famous Leonardo da Vinci art piece from this time was a joint painting with Verrocchio—the dramatic *Baptism of Christ*. While Verrocchio was working on a panel depicting Christ's baptism, Leonardo da Vinci painted an angel holding some garments. Despite his youth, Leonardo da Vinci's

Uncovering Leonardo's Workshop

Amazingly, in 2005, researchers may have discovered the studio of one of history's greatest artists. In January, a group of researchers discovered what might turn out to be Leonardo da Vinci's forgotten workshop. The studio was part of the Santissima Annunziata convent in Florence, Italy. During the Renaissance, nuns sometimes rented rooms to artists. The shop has 500-year-old frescoes on the walls and a secret room where Leonardo da Vinci may have dissected human corpses. Since Leonardo da Vinci's time, this wing of the convent had been split by a wall. Today it is partly owned by the Institute of Military Geography.

According to researchers, proof of the studio is on the walls. Frescoes painted on the walls were work was far better than any of Verrocchio's figures. This painting turned out to be Verrocchio's last. He was ashamed that a far younger man understood the use of colors so much better than he did. From that point on, Verrocchio concentrated on sculpting.

Other works of Leonardo da Vinci from this time have long since been lost. One such exquisite painting was a watercolor of Adam and Eve in the

forgotten and left undisturbed for hundreds of years. One colorful fresco has a missing character in the foreground. The white silhouette bears a striking resemblance to Leonardo da Vinci's angel in *The Annunciation*. Researchers are unsure whether the angel was removed or simply never painted. The walls are also decorated with birds. Several of these paintings are very similar to sketches from the "Atlantic Codex," a 1,286-page collection of Leonardo da Vinci's drawings and writings. Some experts caution that it is still too early to say whether or not the workshop is authentic, but the discoverers are certain that further research will back up their claims.

Garden of Eden. Leonardo da Vinci was commissioned to paint the picture, which was then copied and woven into a tapestry of gold and silver, for the king of Portugal. The painting was last mentioned in the 1540s as being in the house of Ottaviano de' Medici. Another lost piece was an oil painting of Medusa with a coil of serpents on her head. Medusa is a character in Greek mythology. This work was Leonardo da Vinci's first classical painting.

Another lost portrait was of a beautiful, rich, young woman named Ginevra de' Benci. She was born in the summer of 1457, south of Florence. Much like the Medicis, she belonged to a family of bankers who rose to wealth. The family hired Leonardo da Vinci, the promising young artist, to paint her portrait.

The missing painting of Ginevra de' Benci was finally found in the early 1900s, in an obscure art collection. The small painting is only about 15 inches tall. Ginevra de' Benci's sad face is pale, round, and radiant against the dark juniper leaves in the background. The painting exudes a ghostly feeling. A distant light hovers over the thin arms of the trees and glistens on the water.

Ginevra de' Benci's eyes look off in a heavy, distracted gaze. Her smooth, glossy, auburn hair curls in ringlets around her face.

Some believe this portrait was Leonardo da Vinci's first masterpiece. The piece portrays the throwing off of restraints. The ringlets of hair give Ginevra de' Benci liveliness, in contrast to the dark, serious background. Leonardo da Vinci truly captured poetry in this painting, a talent he had not acquired from Verrocchio. Perhaps Leonardo da Vinci was about to throw off his own restraints, as well.

Test Your Knowledge

1 What was Compagnia di San Luca?

    a. A fraternity of Florentine bankers

    b. A fraternity of Florentine painters

    c. A fraternity of Florentine musicians

    d. A fraternity of Florentine merchants

2 *The Annunciation* and *Madonna of the Carnation* share what subject?

    a. Mary

    b. The three wise men

    c. Joseph

    d. Jesus

3 *Baptism of Christ* was a joint project with

    a. Picasso.

    b. Michelangelo.

    c. Verrocchio.

    d. all of the above.

4 Who was Medusa?

    a. A character in a William Shakespeare play

    b. A character in Norse mythology

    c. A character in Roman mythology

    d. A character in Greek mythology

5 What was the profession of Ginevra de' Benci's family?

a. Bankers

b. Lawyers

c. Musicians

d. Poets

ANSWERS: 1. b; 2. a; 3. c; 4. d; 5. a

Leonardo da Vinci's Studio

By 1478, Leonardo da Vinci had set up his own studio in Florence. After ten years as Verrocchio's student, apprentice, and assistant, Leonardo da Vinci was ready to step out on his own. His portrait of Ginevra de' Benci proved that the young artist had found his own style, and he could no longer hide in the master's studio. He took on his first apprentice—Paolo, a teenager from Florence.

During this time, Leonardo da Vinci also received his first commission for a painting as an independent artist. The commission was for a large altarpiece to hang in the chapel of the Palazzo Vecchio, the Capella di San Bernardo. His piece would replace an earlier painting by Bernardo Daddi, showing the Virgin Mary as she appeared in a vision to St. Bernard. Leonardo da Vinci agreed to create a painting with the same theme. He received a cash advance for the project but, for some reason, never delivered the work. No trace of any sketch was ever found. This was the first job Leonardo da Vinci had ever abandoned, and the action damaged his reputation as a painter.

At about the same time, he sketched a very interesting picture in one of his notebooks. The sketch depicted an execution. Shortly before noon on April 26, 1478, a sudden commotion interrupted the Mass in Florence's cathedral. As the sanctuary bell rang, a man in the crowd pulled a knife out of his coat and plunged it into Giuliano de' Medici, the younger brother of Lorenzo de' Medici. Giuliano de' Medici reeled back in pain. Another man joined in and ferociously stabbed him many times. In the end, Giuliano de' Medici's crumpled, lifeless body had been stabbed 19 times.

The assassination—known as the Pazzi Conspiracy—had been ordered by the rich Florentine Pazzi family, in hopes of overthrowing the Medicis. Lorenzo de' Medici was injured in the fight, but managed to escape. Nearby citizens quickly dragged him to safety in the sacristy, as he bled from a wound in his neck.

In all the confusion, the assassins escaped, but the other half of the Pazzi plan had failed. The Pazzis and a group of mercenaries wanted to take over the Palazzo della Signoria—Florence's government building. Jacopo de' Pazzi galloped into the *piazza*, or city square, shouting, "For the people and for freedom!"[9] The doors to the building had already been barred shut, and the town warning bell pealed from the tower.

Bloody revenge followed. The first night, a mass lynching spread throughout the city. The bodies of 20 suspected Pazzi conspirators were hanged from the Signoria's windows. Lorenzo de' Medici stood in one window, a scarf bandaged around his wounded neck. According to some historians, he ordered three life-sized wax figures of himself to be placed in several windows. As his revenge squad ran loose on the streets, he would watch over the city in his moment of triumph. Over the next few days, another 60 conspirators were killed.

Of the four original assassins from the cathedral, three were soon captured. The fourth man, Bernardo di Bandio, managed to escape to Constantinople, but the powerful Medicis had friends everywhere. Within a year, Lorenzo de' Medici received news of Bandio's hiding place, and Lorenzo de' Medici ordered him dragged back to Florence in chains. Bernardo di Bandio was hanged on December 28, 1479.

Leonardo da Vinci witnessed the hanging. He drew a sketch of Bernardo di Bandio dangling from the noose, hands tied behind his back, head limp, and feet unbound. In the top, left corner of his notebook page, Leonardo da Vinci even jotted down what Bernardo di Bandio was wearing at the time of his execution: "Small tan-colored berretta; doublet of black serge; a black jerkin lined; a blue coat lined with fox fur and the color of the jerkin

Leonardo da Vinci witnessed the hanging of Bernardo di Bandio, one of the coconspirators in the assassination of Giuliano de' Medici. He included this sketch of a hanged man in one of his notebooks.

covered with stippled velvet, red and black; black hose." [10] Today Leonardo da Vinci's drawing is the only surviving "news article" of the event.

LEONARDO DA VINCI'S OTHER SIDES

Leonardo da Vinci's second assistant was Tommaso di Giovanni Masini, more commonly known as Zoroastro. Zoroastro ground colors for Leonardo da Vinci. The young assistant was born in 1462 in the village of Petatola, a town in the flatlands between Florence and Prato. He was a jester, a magician, a chemist, and just like Leonardo da Vinci, a vegetarian. In his notebooks, Leonardo da Vinci gave Zoroastro the nickname "Maestro Tommaso." This name probably came from an unusually decorated cloak that Leonardo da Vinci had made for him.

Zoroastro made a unique impression on Leonardo da Vinci. He made strangely brewed concoctions, kept rare reptiles, and painted odd animals with grotesque faces. The young jokester probably inspired Leonardo da Vinci's early work as an engineer. None of Leonardo da Vinci's first technological drawings actually developed into projects, but they certainly got his imagination churning. He drew possible inventions using levers, hoists, and cranes.

One of his drawings was of a machine that could raise the temple of San Giovanni without any damage to the building. Because of frequent flood damage, Leonardo da Vinci believed the temple should be placed on top of steps. Many people who saw Leonardo da Vinci's design believed it could be done.

Leonardo da Vinci also drew a device that could open a prison cell from the inside, by ripping off the iron bars. His interest in this invention most likely came from an experience in his life. Several years earlier, he had been imprisoned for questionable conduct with a young student. He was released, but the event, no doubt, affected him. Some people who saw the drawing believed it had no useful purpose, but was only for mischief.

In addition to these drawings, Leonardo da Vinci designed many more things. He imagined water-powered mills with millstones, grinders, and ovens. He wanted to harness the force of the vortex—the concept of the funnel in a whirlpool or tornado being so strong that nothing could resist it. These early drawings were the first images of one of the great energy principles of Leonardian physics. Leonardo da Vinci used the term *snail shell*, but his drawings eventually became the idea behind the force of screws, drills, and propellers.

Leonardo da Vinci also created drawings of a flying machine. The aircraft had scalloped wings, like a bat, and a fanned out tail, like a bird. The handles could be operated by the pilot, much like a modern-day hang glider.

Leonardo da Vinci was also a poet and a musician. He was friends with the "poets in a hurry." This group of literary people dashed off poems with an on-the-spot, or impromptu, feel. They wrote with a deliberate roughness and used slang vocabulary, much like the rap artists of today. Most of their poems were about poverty, hunger, disappointment, and depression. Some of the poets wrote satire, or political humor. Leonardo da Vinci dabbled in a little of this poetry. His literary friends sometimes wrote about him. Poet Cammelli wrote about Leonardo da Vinci being pained, stressed, and poor. Perhaps his bottega was not doing well at the time.

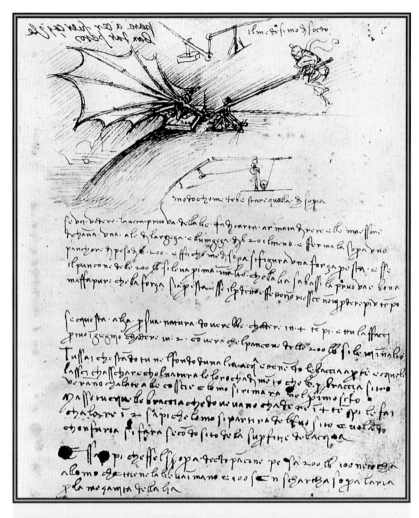

In addition to his incredible artistic talents, Leonardo da Vinci was also a would-be inventor. This design for a flying machine was included in one of his notebooks.

More than poetry, however, Leonardo da Vinci wrote riddles. They had a definite literary and rhythmic quality, much like poems.

Leonardo da Vinci was a brilliant musician. In some circles, he was better known for his musical talent than his painting. He was especially good at playing the lyre—a stringed instrument, much like a violin. The lyre had seven strings. Five strings were played with a horse-hair bow and a finger board to sound different notes. The others were open strings, which could be plucked for a single tone, or used to produce a beat. None of Leonardo da Vinci's compositions survived, but he probably played the light, upbeat carnival music of Florence. Leonardo da Vinci was not, however, a typical artist in many ways. It is possible that he played a more smooth and philosophical tune.

According to some sources, Leonardo da Vinci made his own lyre, mostly of silver, and shaped like a horse's head. Despite its unusual shape, it had an exceptionally full sound. There are no sketches of this lyre in his notebooks, but he did draw many other new types of instruments.

ST. JEROME

"Leonardo, why so troubled?" wrote Cammelli.[11] A downhearted mood was portrayed in the anguished expression of Leonardo da Vinci's *St. Jerome.* St. Jerome was an ancient Greek scholar of the fourth century (300 A.D.–400). He was often featured as the subject of Renaissance art. A spell was placed on him, causing him to wander the Syrian desert alone.

Leonardo da Vinci started the painting around 1480. He showed St. Jerome wasting away, striking himself with a stone. Every muscle in his neck and shoulders was visible. In what is considered Leonardo da Vinci's first anatomical drawing, St. Jerome's face shows intense pain and emotion.

As in all of the St. Jerome paintings of the time, a lion is pictured in the corner. Many mistook Jerome for the saint who won the friendship of a lion by pulling a thorn from his paw. This person, however, was actually San Gerasimo. In Leonardo da Vinci's painting, the lion is probably the artist himself—witnessing the saint's suffering.

LEAVING FLORENCE

Early in 1481, Leonardo da Vinci accepted a new commission to paint an altarpiece. This time, the work was for a rich Augustinian monastery in Scopeto, a village just outside of Florence. For this

Leonardo da Vinci's *St. Jerome* depicted the ancient Greek scholar of the fourth century. In what is considered Leonardo da Vinci's first anatomical drawing, St. Jerome's face shows intense pain and emotion.

job, he began *Adoration of the Magi*—the last and greatest of his early Florentine works. This piece, his largest easel painting, was eight feet tall and almost eight feet wide. The painting told the story of the three wise men who visited the Christ child.

At that time, the magi were among the most popular subjects among Renaissance painters. As always, Leonardo da Vinci put a different twist on his work. He created an amazing group of images inside the painting. Altogether there were 60 people and animals in the crowd, an uncommon feat for an artist.

Once again, Leonardo da Vinci did not finish the painting. By this time, he had earned a reputation as a lazy artist. He often strayed from his work for months at a time, fiddling with colors and other projects. It was probably just as well that he never delivered the painting, however. The monastery was completely demolished in the early 1500s, and the painting probably would have been destroyed with it.

In early 1482, Leonardo da Vinci packed his things and left Florence for Milan, Italy. The reason for his departure is unclear. Lorenzo de' Medici

Studying Linear Perspective

Leonardo da Vinci used linear perspective in his paintings. This mathematical system helps to create the illusion of space and distance on a flat surface. The system originated in Florence, Italy, in the early 1400s. Leonardo da Vinci probably learned the technique while studying as an apprentice.

In order to use linear perspective, an artist must first imagine the picture's surface as an open window through which to view the painted world. He or she must then draw a straight line to represent the horizon. The horizon line runs across the canvas at eye level. This horizontal line is where the sky appears to meet the ground. The painter selects a vanishing point near the center of the horizon line.

Next the artist draws many visual rays, or orthogonal lines, connecting the viewer's eye to the point in the distance. These lines all run toward the vanishing point, like train tracks appear to come together in the distance. The artist uses the visual rays to align the edges of walls and buildings. Through linear perspective, objects in a painting appear to have actual depth and dimension.

Try using linear perspective to create your own drawing. See how the picture comes to life.

may have sent him to Milan as an example of Florence's artistic talent, or perhaps he left with his head hung low, carrying a stack of unfinished art and the pain of failure.

One thing is certain. Leonardo da Vinci went to Milan as an engineer, not as an artist. Shortly before he left, he made a list of his Florentine works, as a portfolio of his career, but in a letter of introduction to the duke of Milan, he described himself as an inventor. "I therefore make bold, without ill-will to any, to offer my skills to Your Excellency," he wrote, "and to acquaint Your Lordship with my secrets, and will be glad to demonstrate effectively all these things. . . ." [12]

Leonardo da Vinci included in his letter a list of his "secrets," especially for war. "I have methods for making very light and strong bridges," he stated, "useful whether pursuing or evading the enemy." In another part of the letter, he wrote, "I have certain types of cannon, extremely easy to carry, which fire out small stones, almost as if it were a hailstorm . . ." [13] He offered ideas for making underground tunnels that could even wind under rivers. He claimed to have created ideas for armored cars and many other things. He did remember that he was also an artist. "In painting," he wrote, "I can do everything that is possible to do." [14] In conclusion, he offered to begin work on a bronze horse statue for the duke's family.

He carefully wrapped up his portfolio and letters. He was, no doubt, hoping that Milan would hold greater glory for him than Florence. He put the papers and drawings in his saddle bag, and his clay figurines in a traveling chest. With his lyre case in hand, he began his journey toward a new life.

Test Your Knowledge

1 For how long was young Leonardo a student and apprentice to Verrocchio?
a. Five years
b. Ten years
c. Three years
d. Seven years

2 By what name was the assassination attempt on the Medici brothers known?
a. The Duomo Conspiracy
b. The San Lorenzo Conspiracy
c. The Medici Conspiracy
d. The Pazzi Conspiracy

3 What was the term Leonardo da Vinci used for the force behind the motion of screws, drills, and propellers?
a. Twister
b. Tortoise shell
c. Snail shell
d. Wind tunnel

4 What modern-day machine did Leonardo da Vinci's flying machine resemble?
a. A hang glider
b. A kite
c. A parachute
d. A hot-air balloon

5 In some circles, aside from his painting, Leonardo da Vinci was known for what?

a. Engineering talent

b. Musical talent

c. Poetic talent

d. Cooking ability

ANSWERS: 1. b; 2. d; 3. c; 4. a; 5. b

In Milan

Leonardo da Vinci copied a passage out of Dante's *Inferno*. It read, "Lying in a featherbed will not bring you fame, nor staying beneath the quilt, and he who uses up his life without achieving fame leaves no more vestige of himself on earth than smoke in the air or foam upon the water."[15] Perhaps these were

Leonardo da Vinci's thoughts on his journey from Florence to Milan. The trip was about 180 miles. On horseback, it would have taken about a week. A famous musician named Atalante Migliorotti traveled with Leonardo da Vinci. Zoroastro also may have made the trip.

In 1482, Milan was a growing city with a population of about 80,000 people. The town was larger than Florence, but lacked its commercial and political importance. The duchy of Milan reached south from the Alps, across the Lombard plain, and from the port of Genoa on the western coast to the edge of the Republic of Venice on the east. The kingdom stood in the center of trade and invasion routes from the north, contributing to its history of warfare. Over the years, Milan had become famous for manufacturing weapons. It made perfect sense, then, that Leonardo da Vinci would try to sell his ideas for military equipment.

Even at age 30, Leonardo da Vinci was still wide-eyed and awestruck by the massiveness of the city. Most of the buildings were constructed of red brick, making them stand out against the azure blue sky. Tall walls with seven gates and a wide moat surrounded the city. Each of the seven gates had its own guard tower. Inside the city walls, the duke's castle was just as impressive. The castle had walls and towers of its own, as if it were a city in itself.

The Duke of Milan, Ludovico Sforza, was an ambitious and scheming man, who also loved music. Leonardo da Vinci was known throughout Italy as a composer and performer on his lyre. He had won a music competition in Florence, making him one of the best performers around. In Ludovico Sforza's court, music was extremely important. Clearly, the Duke of Milan was far more interested in Leonardo da Vinci's ability to entertain than in his engineering abilities.

Ludovico Sforza ran a lively court with elaborate plays and pageants. He especially enjoyed mysteries about spies and assassins. He hosted elegant balls and masquerades, always accompanied by festive music. Leonardo da Vinci would be a wonderful addition to the duke's performers.

IN THE COURTS

Leonardo da Vinci served as the master of court festivities. He designed colorful sets and costumes.

The corner tower of Sforza Castle is shown here. Ludovico Sforza, the Duke of Milan, served as a patron to Leonardo da Vinci, in Milan, Italy.

He probably remembered the tricks of set design that he had witnessed in the theaters of Florence. He also directed and performed the music.

In February 1489, the granddaughter of the king of Naples came to Milan to marry Ludovico Sforza's nephew. Huge tapestries and wreaths hung throughout the city. An enormous celebration was planned. No expense was spared. Even the cooks and servants wore elaborate costumes of silk and satin. Ludovico Sforza assigned Leonardo da Vinci the task of decorating the courtyard of the castle. Leonardo da Vinci built pillars made from twigs and covered them with a roof of leaves. The leaves were so tightly woven and beautifully trimmed, they looked more like a painting than actual leaves.

Leonardo da Vinci also organized the entertainment for the guests. He called the performance "Paradise." The actors wore dazzling golden cloaks. They rode into the hall on great horses, while dancers leaped beside them. Suddenly a curtain covering one side of the hall rose up. The guests stared in wonder at what appeared to be the heavens—twinkling stars and glittering planets. The planets began to move above the guests. The gods, after whom they were named—Venus, Mars, Jupiter—all flew across the sky dressed in full costume. The audience gasped in astonishment and delight.

In addition to his court responsibilities, the duke asked Leonardo da Vinci to design some new canals for the city and to modernize the old ones. Meanwhile, Leonardo da Vinci's skill as a painter certainly was not overlooked. Ludovico Sforza also kept him busy as the court artist. Leonardo da Vinci created portraits of various members of the royal court. One of the duke's favorites was a painting of his mistress, Cecilia Gallerani. The painting became known as *The Lady with an Ermine* because she held a pet ermine, a type of weasel, in her arms.

These accomplishments alone would have made Leonardo da Vinci famous, but his most important commission was the bronze monument he had promised to the duke in his letter. The equestrian statue would honor the duke's father, Francesco, "The Thug." One of Verrocchio's most famous creations was a similar bronze statue of another famous warrior—Bartolommeo Colleoni. Once again, however, Leonardo da Vinci planned to outdo his former teacher. He wanted to make this

Da Vinci's *Lady with an Ermine* depicts Cecilia Gallerani, Ludovico Sforza's mistress. She holds a pet ermine, a type of weasel, in her arms.

horse a massive 24 feet high, and he would cast it out of a single piece of bronze—some 160,000 pounds of metal. Such a feat would be difficult, even with today's more modern methods, but Leonardo da Vinci's ambitions knew no limits.

He needed to create a fiery design that symbolized pride and power. He spent countless hours drawing many pictures, using different horses as models. He also made special molds that would be used for the casting, and four furnaces for melting the bronze. In the fall of 1493, he finished a full-scale model in clay. The model was displayed in the palace courtyard for all to see. Anyone who laid eyes on the horse, admired it, but, once again, the work would never be finished. This time, unrest in the world got in the way.

LUDOVICO SFORZA'S AMBITION

Although Ludovico Sforza acted as ruler of Milan, he was not actually the true duke. He had assumed the role of duke for his nephew Gian Galeazzo, who came into power when he was much too young to actually rule. The young ruler grew up to be weak and unfit for the throne. Ludovico Sforza wanted to take over Milan, but he feared the king of Naples would frown on it.

Sforza decided to ask for help from the French king, Charles VIII. He told the king to go ahead and take the crown of Naples. Secretly, Sforza knew this would remove any threat to himself, allowing him to take his rightful spot as duke of Milan.

King Charles took Ludovico Sforza's advice. In September 1494, he crossed over into Italy with a force of some 50,000 well-trained soldiers. He won an easy victory in Naples. The city surrendered without a drop of blood being spilled. Much to Sforza's unexpected delight, his nephew fell seriously ill. He died in October, and his merciless uncle immediately seized the crown.

Meanwhile, in Florence, Piero de' Medici, the cowardly son of Lorenzo de' Medici, had been ruling. When he heard that King Charles was on the move to take over parts of Italy, he rushed to the French camp and made a friendly treaty with the king. Furious at Piero de' Medici's perceived weakness, the people of Florence revolted against him. Piero de' Medici and his brothers fled the city, bringing an end to the long era of Medici rule.

In Milan, Ludovico Sforza was quite pleased with this news. If he could find a way to get rid of King Charles, he could take over Florence and Naples and become the supreme ruler in Italy, but he would have to turn against his ally. About this time, Spain and Germany formed an alliance with Venice and the pope, to seal off the French in Italy. Ludovico Sforza saw his opportunity. He joined the alliance against King Charles. Suddenly, six months after taking over Naples, the French king was retreating up the Italian peninsula. He made it back to France just in time.

Even though Ludovico Sforza seemed to be stepping into the limelight, Leonardo da Vinci's life was become increasingly bleak. There was no further talk about the great bronze horse sculpture. The bronze that was to be used for the statue had been used to make cannons. Worse yet, Ludovico Sforza stopped making payments to his artist. It seemed the new duke had little time for art.

Desperate for money, Leonardo da Vinci wrote the duke a letter. "If your Lordship thought that I had money," he explained, "your Lordship was deceived, because I had to feed six men for thirty-six months." [16]

Finally, at the end of 1495, Leonardo da Vinci's fortunes improved. The duke commissioned him to do a wall painting in the dining room of the Convent of the Santa Maria delle Grazie. His subject was to be the Last Supper of Jesus and the Disciples.

For Leonardo da Vinci, this story was more than just a decorative mural. It was a moment of intense drama, when Christ revealed to his disciples that one of them was a betrayer. Leonardo da Vinci wanted to keep the attention focused on the central figure in the story—Jesus Christ. He also wanted to bring out all of the tense emotions of the others. The background should not distract from the story.

In a note to himself, Leonardo da Vinci wrote:

Make your work in keeping with your purpose and design: that is, when you make your figure you should consider carefully who it is and what you wish it to be doing . . . that figure is most praiseworthy which by his actions best expresses the passions of the soul.[17]

After much thought, Leonardo da Vinci began his painting. Most murals at that time were frescoes. This kind of wall art was made by painting water

This restoration of Leonardo da Vinci's *The Last Supper* took more than 20 years to complete. This painting has remained one of the artist's most profound works.

colors on fresh plaster. The colors soaked into the wall, and the artwork lasted a long time, but the painting had to be done with deliberate speed, because the plaster dried so quickly.

Leonardo da Vinci liked to take his time when he painted. He wanted to make retouches and changes, so he decided to use an oil and tempera paint that dried slowly. Sometimes he spent long days at his work. He would go into the dining room early in the morning and stay at work from sunrise until night. He would not even pause to eat or drink. At other times, three of four days would pass when he would not even touch the painting.

Leonardo da Vinci explained his work habits this way: "It is a good plan every now and then to go away and have a little relaxation," he wrote, "for then when you come back to the work, your judgment will be surer."[18] It took him three years to finish the piece. Slowly the beautiful faces, breath-taking gestures, and passionate emotion came to life. For centuries, Leonardo da Vinci's *The Last Supper* has remained one of his most profound works of art.

Today people can see very little of the original painting. As it turns out, the decision to use oil paints was a disaster. The wall was damp, and soon after the painting was finished, it began to peel. Over the years, the mural has been restored many times. Sometimes the restoration did more harm than good, but the magnificent emotion of the original painting still manages to shine through to grab the attention and emotion of the viewer.

Test Your Knowledge

1 What was the population of Milan in 1482?
a. About 20,000 people
b. About 50,000 people
c. About 100,000 people
d. About 80,000 people

2 Over the years, Milan had become famous for
a. the number of artists it produced.
b. manufacturing weapons.
c. its wonderful Italian cuisine.
d. its magnificent architecture.

3 What function did Leonardo da Vinci serve
in Ludovico Sforza's court?
a. Official court musician
b. Court jester
c. Master of court festivities
d. Court poet

4 What was the subject of the wall painting
Leonardo da Vinci was commissioned to
paint in 1495?
a. The Last Supper of Jesus and the Disciples
b. The Crucifixion
c. Mary holding a dying Jesus in her arms
d. The Annunciation

5 How long did it take Leonardo da Vinci to complete *The Last Supper*?

a. Ten years

b. Seven years

c. Five years

d. Three years

ANSWERS: 1. d; 2. b; 3. c; 4. a; 5. d

Going Home

In the spring of 1499, Leonardo da Vinci's career was flourishing. To make up for the unpaid salary for the bronze horse that never came to fruition, Ludovico Sforza gave Leonardo da Vinci a lovely vineyard outside of Milan. Clustered vines twisted up the hillside, and the sweet smell of grapes floated on the breeze. This sight, no doubt, reminded Leonardo da Vinci of his childhood home in Vinci.

During the summer, he once again studied mechanics. He also brushed up on his geometry and mathematics. Finally the duke appointed him to the post of engineer. The job must have been a wonderful accomplishment, for Leonardo da Vinci took great pride in his inventions and ideas.

He inspected the city walls. He stood at a distance, eyes squinted, rubbing his chin. He made suggestions for strengthening the stone fortresses. Meanwhile Lodovico Sforza worried about another French invasion. King Charles had died and the new king, Louis XII, was determined to try again to invade Naples. This time, he would take Milan as a stronghold in the north. Ludovico Sforza wanted to keep the city as safe from attack as possible.

Again the duke needed outside help. He traveled to Germany to win the emperor's support against King Louis. While he was gone, King Louis made his move. He led his troops to Naples, and then on to Milan. Without the duke, the stone-walled city fell to the French without even a struggle. French archers roamed around the palace courtyard and used Leonardo da Vinci's great horse model for target practice.

The fall of Milan was a terrible blow for Leonardo da Vinci. His 17-year career in Milan was over. The French had no use for him. With nothing else to do, he decided to leave the city. In December 1499, he packed his belongings. He sold whatever he could not move and wisely invested the money. He set off for Florence by a roundabout way, through northern Italy.

RETURN TO FLORENCE

Leonardo da Vinci made several stops on his trip. First he traveled to Mantua, where he stayed for several months. During his visit, he sketched Isabella d'Este, the beautiful wife of Mantua's ruler. He then journeyed to Venice. The people there welcomed him with excitement. He helped the engineers plan a defense for the city against a possible Turkish attack. Finally, at the end of April 1500, he was ready to go home to Florence.

Much had changed since he had left Florence 18 years earlier. His old teacher, Verrocchio, had died. His fellow apprentices had become great artists.

When Leonardo da Vinci left Milan, he made numerous stops in northern Italy, on his way back to Florence. In Mantua, he sketched this portrait of Isabella d'Este, the beautiful wife of Mantua's ruler.

He entered the city a homeless wanderer, but he was confident his friends would invite him back into their circle, as an established artist. To his relief, the painters greeted him with thrilled smiles and energetic hand shakes. Leonardo da Vinci had brought a good name to his native town, and they were happy to welcome him home.

Soon after Leonardo da Vinci's arrival, the Servite monks of Florence commissioned artist Filippino Lippi to paint an altarpiece. This painter had finished one of Leonardo da Vinci's earlier abandoned projects. Leonardo da Vinci told a friend, "I would have gladly undertaken such a work."[19] When Filippino Lippi heard this, he graciously stepped aside and let Leonardo da Vinci take over the job. The monks were happy to have such a distinguished artist do their painting. They even offered him a place to stay.

Leonardo da Vinci decided to paint the Virgin Mary and St. Anne with the baby Jesus. He began drawing a first sketch in chalk. One historian wrote that his sketch "not only filled all artists with wonder, but when it was finished, men and women, young and old, continued for two days to crowd into the room where it was exhibited . . . and all were astonished at its excellence."[20]

Unfortunately the preliminary sketch was as far as Leonardo da Vinci ever took the project. The disappointed monks had to get Filippino Lippi to finish the work—again. Other important people of Florence were trying to get Leonardo da Vinci to paint for them, but they had little success. He painted *The Virgin with the Yarn Winder* for the secretary of King Louis of France, but he did not finish the painting of Isabella d'Este he had sketched in Mantua. Isabella's agent wrote, "[He's] working hard at geometry and has no patience with his brush. His mathematical experiments have so distracted him from painting," he continued, "that the sight of his brush puts him out of temper."[21]

SEARCHING FOR ANSWERS

Throughout his life, Leonardo da Vinci led an endless search for knowledge. He wanted to discover the hidden laws of nature. He desired to unlock the mysteries of the mind. "The natural desire of good men is knowledge," he wrote.[22] As he grew older, he became absorbed in finding the meaning of things. He put aside his painting, which was only a mirror of nature.

He became depressed about life. Many of his great works seemed to have ended in failure. His mural *The Battle of Anghiari* had stopped until the plaster could be tested. His painting *The Last Supper* was peeling off the wall. His experiments with flight had failed, and he never wrote hopefully about them again. With each passing day, he only had more questions instead of answers. "While I thought that I was learning how to live," he cried, "I have been learning how to die."[23]

By the spring of 1506, his unhappiness became almost unbearable. He was 54 years old, and all his years of work had brought him no security. He constantly worried about money. Just when he was about to despair, he received a letter from Milan that could solve all his problems.

After the overthrow of Ludovico Sforza, Charles d'Amboise became governor of Milan. He was also marshal of France and grand admiral of the French fleet. He was a man who appreciated art. He had no doubt seen Leonardo da Vinci's great horse and his painting of *The Last Supper*. In May 1506, the governor invited Leonardo da Vinci to come to Milan for several months.

Leonardo da Vinci was ready to go, but the city council of Florence stopped him. They knew

Leonardo da Vinci's track record of unfinished work. They feared *The Battle of Anghiari* would be added to the list. At the end of May, the council drew up a new contract. Leonardo da Vinci agreed to pay the city a deposit. If he never returned to finish his mural, he would lose his money.

The painter's return to Milan was a triumph. Charles d'Amboise kept him busy with many projects, and the two seemed to get along well. In August, Charles d'Amboise wrote to the council of Florence asking to extend Leonardo da Vinci's stay in Milan. At first, Florence agreed. The French had enormous power in Italy, but in September, when Charles d'Amboise asked for another extension, the council refused. Florence demanded Leonardo da Vinci's return.

A final decision was made by King Louis XII of France. King Louis had been planning another trip to Italy, through Milan. Charles d'Amboise knew about this expedition. He sent King Louis a painting of the Virgin Mary that Leonardo da Vinci had recently finished. The king was deeply impressed.

In January 1507, King Louis called in his ambassador to Florence. "It is time for your council to do me a favor," he said. "Write to them that I wish to employ the painter Master Leonardo, who is now in Milan."

The ambassador wrote a letter to the council. King Louis followed it with an even stronger letter. This time, the council dared not refuse. In May, King Louis arrived in Milan. He asked Leonardo da Vinci to become the royal painter and engineer of France.

Finally Leonardo da Vinci began to feel appreciated. He once again moved on to his vineyard property outside the city. He was paid regularly, for a change. In painting, he completed only a few small pictures of the Madonna (Virgin Mary), but he spent much time working as an engineer, an architect, and a manager of arts. As he had done for Ludovico Sforza, he designed great devices for pageants. He planned a beautiful garden, bubbling with fountains and dotted with trees. He even created hidden water jets that sprayed visitors as they passed by. The garden also housed windmills that powered musical instruments. A gentle breeze would strike up a tune.

Leonardo da Vinci only had one interruption in his duties in Milan. He had to return to Florence for a short time. His father had died in 1504, and there was some trouble settling his estate. During his stay, he was free to travel and do scientific research. He took trips into the mountains. He studied the fossil shells buried there, just as he had done as a child. He noticed that not all the shells were at the top or on the sides of the mountains. Some fossils were buried deep inside. These fossils had been exposed by streams that eroded the rock away.

Leonardo da Vinci concluded that the fossils could not have been set by one great flood, as was first believed from the Bible. "Here a doubt arises," he noted, "whether the Flood, which came at the time of Noah, was universal or not, and this would seem not to have been the case."[24]

Leonardo da Vinci's most amazing scientific discoveries were in anatomical studies. Anatomy is the study of the living bodies and how they work. At the time, there was a religious ban on dissecting human corpses, but the law was rarely enforced.

By the end of the 1400s, many artists could study the inner workings of the body in the dissecting chamber.

At first, Leonardo da Vinci carefully watched doctors perform autopsies. Then he began making his own dissections. He purchased a fine set of surgical knives and instruments. As he cut away parts of the body, he drew detailed sketches of everything he saw. In the beginning, he simply wanted to learn more about the human body so that he could paint it more realistically. He soon wanted to uncover the answers of life itself. "And would that it might please our Creator," he decided, "that I were able to reveal the nature of man and his customs even as I describe his figure."[25] He made hundreds of drawings of muscles, bones, blood vessels, and organs. His sketches are so clear and accurate, they are still used in anatomy books today.

He was particularly fascinated by the heart. He disagreed with medical opinions of the time on how the heart worked. He found it was "a vessel formed of thick muscle, vivified and nourished by the artery and vein."[26]

He made casts of the aorta—the main artery that carries blood away from the heart. To do this, he used the aorta of an ox. He filled it with wax and made a plaster impression of it. He then blew glass into the mold. In so doing, he made a glass mold of the heart. Through the glass mold, he could study the movement of pulsing blood as it passed through the heart. "All the veins and arteries proceed from the heart," he noted. The beating heart produces "a wave of blood in all the veins."[27]

Leonardo da Vinci's science entailed more than the study of the human body. He also compared his findings with animals. "In fact," he concluded, "man does not vary from the animals except in what is accidental."[28] He also studied the solar system. He drew illustrations of plants that few artists could ever match.

In addition, Leonardo da Vinci devoted one whole notebook to the growth and development of a human embryo. He was the first person to dissect a female womb and to draw the unborn child inside of it. Leonardo da Vinci's amazing contributions to science, however, would soon come to an end.

FASCINATED BY "THINGS"

Leonardo da Vinci may have earned a reputation as an artist who rarely finished his work, but he was still considered a great talent. He was simply too busy to paint. Instead he wrote long essays on physics, such as force and motion. He made a special magnifying glass with which to observe the moon. He experimented with weights and commented, "Every weight seems to fall toward the center of the earth by the shortest way."[29]

Leonardo da Vinci, the engineer, returned to his study of screws, levers, and gears. This time, he put his ideas to the test. He created a lens grinder, a spinning machine, a mechanical cloth loom, and an automatic printing press that could be worked by a one person. Everywhere he went, he carried his sketchbook, but instead of drawing people, he sketched whatever fascinated him—workshops, mills, rocks, farm workers, horses, and wagons. He was caught up in all of the "things" around him. He wanted to know how they worked and how he could make them better.

For a short time, he joined an army training camp as an architect and engineer. He disliked war, however, and quit after ten months. Back in Florence, he decided to try to solve another war problem. For nine years, Florence had been at war with Pisa. The Florentine army seized Pisa, but the rebel vassals were able to avoid surrender by bringing supplies across the Arno River to the citizens. Leonardo da Vinci had studied hydraulics, water, and waterways years before. He came up with an idea.

He believed the Florentines could cut off the supply route by building a canal. The canal would

Leonardo's Inventions

During his lifetime, Leonardo da Vinci's scientific discoveries and mechanical inventions went unnoticed. His notebooks were not published until hundreds of years after his death. As an inventor, Leonardo da Vinci had an incredible gift for insight. Even with little schooling, he could imagine how to make great inventions work.

Not all of Leonardo da Vinci's inventions were viable, but some of his ideas were brilliant forerunners of the machines of the future. One of these ideas was the automobile. Leonardo da Vinci's auto was powered by two huge springs and steered by a bar that moved the rear wheels. Remember, gasoline-powered engines would not be invented until the 1860s.

divert the river away from Pisa. Eventually the city would run out of supplies and would be forced to surrender. The idea took too long and became too costly. When the rainy season began, all work on the canal stopped.

Leonardo da Vinci was not discouraged. He would try something else with the canal. He suggested that workers could turn the canal stretch between

Leonardo da Vinci also designed a self-propelled ship. The ship would moved by paddle wheels, which were mounted on crankshafts. He imagined men turning the cranks to make the wheels turn in the water. A steam-powered paddle wheel was not introduced in America until 1787.

Another one of Leonardo da Vinci's inventions was a machine gun. His gun had three sets of cannons. He designed them mounted to a carriage wheel, so they could be rotated. As one set fired, a second set cooled, and a third set could be loaded. This method was similar to the machine gun Richard Gatling designed in 1861.

Florence and Pisa into a workable waterway for peacetime. Citizens could draw water from the reservoirs when the river ran low. "This will fertilize the country," he wrote. "And Prato, Pistoia, and Pisa, together with Florence, will have a yearly revenue of more than 200,000 ducats.[30] Leonardo da Vinci even designed a giant earthmover. A chain of buckets, operated by a winch and cogwheels, would dig the canal, instead of workers. Unfortunately nothing came of this idea, either. Leonardo da Vinci, however, was now recognized as both a brilliant engineer and painter.

ONE PAINTING FOR FLORENCE

Eager to reward their native genius, the Florence city council asked him to paint a large mural on one of the walls of the council chamber. The theme would be the Battle of Anghiari. In this battle, Francesco Sforza led the Florentine army to victory over the soldiers of Milan. Leonardo da Vinci was anxious to paint a "real" battle, not the soft, fairy-tale battles most painters had done. During his ten months with the military, he had observed the bitterness of war firsthand.

He first wrote down what the battle should look like. He imagined:

> Let the air be full of arrows going in various directions . . . let the balls shot from the guns have a train of smoke following their course . . . show the mark where a fallen man has been dragged through the dust which has become changed to bloodstained mire, and round about in the half-liquid earth. Make the beaten and conquered pale with brows raised and knit together and full of the lines of pain . . . show someone using his hand as a shield for his terrified eyes . . . let others be crying out with their mouths wide open, and fleeing away. . . . Make the dead, some half buried in the dust, others with the dust all mingled with the oozing blood and changing into crimson mud. . . . Show other in the death agony grinding their teeth and rolling their eyes, with clenched fists.[31]

As usual, he spent months drawing many sketches. He made fiery horses with flared nostrils and reared front legs. Men surrounded by pieces of armor fought

Leonardo da Vinci's sketched *The Battle of Anghiari* before he began painting it. He made fiery horses with flared nostrils and reared front legs. Men surrounded by pieces of armor fought and struggled.

and struggled. The action took place on an arched bridge. On one side, he pictured the cavalry riding in. On the other side, soldiers battled on foot.

In October 1503, he started a full-size drawing, or cartoon, that could be copied onto the wall. The council was a little nervous about the slow pace. In

May 1504, they drew up a contract. The city would continue to give Leonardo da Vinci regular pay, but the cartoon drawing had to be finished by February 1505. For once, Leonardo da Vinci met the terms.

He finally transferred the drawing onto the wall and began to paint. Almost immediately, however, he encountered serious problems. The drying material he mixed with the plaster darkened his colors and dried much too quickly. Some bad linseed oil, which he had purchased from a dishonest merchant, would not dry at all. The colors started to run. Somehow he managed to finish the center section of the painting, a tense battle scene, but once he realized his work was ruined, he stopped and refused to finish it. Even the damaged work, however, was worthy of praise. In 1549, one visitor wrote to a friend about Leonardo da Vinci's mural. "Take a [good] look at a group of horses which will appear a miraculous thing to you."[32]

While Leonardo da Vinci was struggling with his damaged paints, a Florentine merchant commissioned him for another painting. This work would become his best-known painting and probably the most famous in the world.

Test Your Knowledge

1 To make up for the unpaid salary for the bronze horse that never came to fruition, Ludovico Sforza gave Leonardo da Vinci
   a. his own art studio.
   b. a vineyard.
   c. a new commission.
   d. several assistants.

2 What event caused the end of Leonardo da Vinci's 17-year career in Milan?
   a. The Hundred Years' War
   b. The end of the Renaissance
   c. The fall of Milan
   d. The naming of a new pope

3 In addition to his work as a brilliant artist, Leonardo da Vinci was also known as
   a. an engineer.
   b. a song writer.
   c. a poet.
   d. a craftsman.

4 Who did the Florentine army defeat in the Battle of Anghiari?
   a. Soldiers of Pisa
   b. Soldiers of the Vatican
   c. Soldiers of Venice
   d. Soldiers of Milan

5 What caused Leonardo da Vinci to stop working on his painting of the Battle of Anghiari?

a. Damaged paint

b. Laziness

c. Lack of money

d. Disagreements with the Duke of Milan

ANSWERS: 1. b; 2. c; 3. a; 4. d; 5. a

Taking Flight

Leonardo da Vinci soon began working on a portrait of the young wife of a Florentine merchant. Her name was Madonna, or Mona, Lisa del Giocondo. He painted her sitting peacefully with her hands folded in front of her. A gentle smile barely lifts her smooth cheeks. One artist later described the painting as "an extraordinary example of how art can imitate nature." He continued:

> The eyes possess the moist luster, and the nose the fine nostrils, rosy and tender, as seen in life . . . the mouth, with its red lips, and the scarlet cheeks seem not color but living flesh. To look closely at her throat, you might imagine that the pulse was beating.[33]

The *Mona Lisa* was a landmark in portraits. Leonardo da Vinci had brought his painting to life like no one else other had ever done. His picture became the model of a true Renaissance portrait. It had captured the spirit of humanism—a philosophy of man for his own sake rather than as an object or a creation of God. This painting echoed the current thoughts bouncing around Florence, among the well-known thinkers of the time.

Leonardo da Vinci struggled to capture the subject's personality and feelings. He embraced the technical problems of painting and worked to solve them. He tested light and shade, skin tones, and textures. He labored with the *Mona Lisa* for three years before he finished it.

Leonardo da Vinci's *Mona Lisa*, one of his most famous portraits, depicts the wife of a young Florentine merchant. He worked on the painting for three years before finishing it.

Meanwhile he continued to master the imitation of nature in other paintings, as well. In order to create a lifelike image, he studied the world around him, took notes, and played with sketches. He observed how shadows fell. Some shadows had sharp edges, while others were fuzzy or foggy. A shadow was never solid black. It had shades of lighter and darker colors. He also watched people's gestures. "Action may show what the figure has in mind," he wrote.[34] He carefully studied how people acted when they argued, laughed, and talked. He quickly found out that a painter's imagination is constantly at work.

BECOMING A BIRD

From an early age, Leonardo da Vinci had dreamed of flying. All of his observations of nature made this dream come alive in him. He was determined to make it a reality. At first, he began watching and taking notes on the flight of birds. He studied the bone structure of bird wings and experimented with larger, similar-looking models. He wanted to write a book about birds, to catalog all his findings. The book would be divided into four parts. In the first

Mona Lisa Stolen!

On August 21, 1911, someone casually strolled into the Salon Carré of the Louvre in Paris. He waited until no one was watching, lifted the *Mona Lisa* off the wall, and walked out of the museum with it. It was the art theft of the century.

The famous painting was stolen on Monday morning, but no one realized it was missing until Tuesday at noon. Immediately the section chief at the museum made a frantic call to the captain of the guards. The captain rushed to tell the curator, who telephoned the Paris Prefect of Police (head of the Paris Police Department). By early afternoon, 60 inspectors and more than 100 policemen had hurried to the Louvre. They bolted the doors and began questioning all the visitors.

For the entire week, police searched every closet and corner. They combed the crime scene room by room and floor by floor, covering all 49 acres of the Louvre. By the end of the search, Inspector Louis Lepine was able to piece together a reconstruction of the crime, but had no real leads on the whereabouts of the criminal.

The theft was front-page news in every major newspaper across the globe. Each reporter had his own idea of what happened to the painting. Some claimed it had been burned. Others believed it had been tossed into the ocean. In the weeks following the disappearance, rewards were posted for any information that would lead to an arrest. For two years, the *Mona Lisa* remained missing.

Then, in November 1913, a letter that changed everything arrived at the office of a Florentine antique dealer. The letter was from a former Louvre employee—Italian carpenter Vincent Perugia. Perugia hated the French and believed the painting belonged to Italy. The antique dealer promptly had the carpenter arrested. Police found the *Mona Lisa* near her birthplace of four centuries earlier, hidden in the humble apartment of her kidnapper. Today *Mona Lisa* again rests in the Louvre, under much tighter security. She receives millions of visitors each year.

part, he would write about beating wings and how they work. The second section would focus on how wings used wind to keep the bird in flight, without beating. The third part could discuss the flight of all creatures, not just birds. In the last part, he would explain the mechanical action of the bird's movements. He would show, for example, how a bird spreads its tail and flaps its wings quickly before landing, to slow down.

He dissected countless birds and bats to see how the muscles moved. At the end of all his research, he planned to attempt an actual flight. Leonardo da Vinci's investigations were spread out over a long period. During his studies, he designed different machines. He sketched a plan for a parachute made of starched linen. Next to it, he wrote, "[A man could lower] himself down from any great height without sustaining any injury."[35] He also drew a contraption that looked like a helicopter.

His final plan, however, was to build a great bird in which a person could fly. He thought if he could increase the size of the bird to hold a man, it would surely work. He never learned, however, that in proportion, a bird's bones are much lighter than a

In the drawing shown here, Leonardo da Vinci designed what was thought by some to be the first helicopter.

person's. A great deal of power would be needed to lift a person and a machine into the air. Still, Leonardo da Vinci was centuries ahead of his time in many of his thoughts and ideas.

He built many models of his flight machines, some of them quite large. He worked on his projects in secrecy, hoping when the time came, he could give the world an amazing surprise. In a note to himself, he wrote:

> Close up with boards the large room above, and make the model large and high, and you will have space upon the roof above . . . if you stand upon the roof at the side of the tower, the men at work in the cupola will not see you.[36]

He used all sorts of materials. He fashioned light fir wood and cane together for the wing frames. For the skin, he tried starched cloth, paper, and parchment. He even padded the joints with leather. Sometime in 1505, it is possible that Leonardo da Vinci put his "bird" to the test. He wrote in one of his notebooks, "The great bird will take its first flight upon the back of the great swan, filling the whole world with amazement and filling all records with its fame."[37] No one knows for sure if he actually tried his flying machine. If he did, it is safe to say, he was not successful. Another 400 years would pass before humans would conquer flight. Leonardo da Vinci, however, was certainly the fore-runner to modern flight.

Test Your Knowledge

1 Leonardo da Vinci's *Mona Lisa* captured the spirit of
a. realism.
b. religion.
c. humanism.
d. existentialism.

2 Leonardo da Vinci wanted to write a book about what subject?
a. Poetry
b. Birds
c. Art
d. Machinery

3 When might Leonardo da Vinci have tested his flying machine?
a. 1505
b. 1501
c. 1455
d. 1555

4 What did Leonardo da Vinci do to see how muscles moved?
a. Worked in a morgue
b. Dissected frogs
c. Examined human cadavers
d. Dissected birds and bats

5 How many years after Leonardo da Vinci's experiments did humans conquer flight?

a. 500 years

b. 200 years

c. 400 years

d. 1,000 years

ANSWERS: 1. c; 2. b; 3. a; 4. d; 5. c

Entering the Great Sea

Pope Julius II of Rome was a great politician and a scheming man. In 1509, he joined an alliance with Germany, Spain, and France against the Republic of Venice. When King Charles of Milan took to the battlefield, using maps Leonardo da Vinci had made for his campaign, Venice quickly surrendered.

115

After the war was over, Pope Julius did the same thing Ludovico Sforza had done to France. He joined his enemy, Venice, together with Spain and the Swiss, and planned to drive the French out of Italy. In February 1511, King Charles died. One year later, the French surrendered Milan. Suddenly, Leonardo da Vinci was thrown out of his privileged position.

In February 1513, Pope Julius died of a fever. He was succeeded by Giovanni de' Medici—one of the three sons of Lorenzo de' Medici. The new pope took the name Leo X. The first thing Pope Leo did was to bring his brother, Giuliano de' Medici, to Rome. Giuliano de' Medici loved magic, arts, and science, and Leonardo da Vinci desperately needed a new supporter for his career. So he decided to go to Rome. On September 24, 1513, Leonardo da Vinci left his vineyard home in Milan on another journey of uncertainty.

LIFE IN ROME

In December 1513, Leonardo da Vinci stood in a magnificent garden on Vatican Hill. He looked out across the grassy plains and low rolling hills around

Rome. Here, in the Palace of Belvedere, he found his new home.

Leonardo da Vinci's new supporter, Giuliano de' Medici, was more interested in magic tricks than in painting. He was captivated by fancy devices and novelty toys. He put Leonardo da Vinci in a workshop, to make distorted mirrors and other sorts of trick items. Leonardo da Vinci spent much of his time building the machines that would make the toys. One of those machines, the first of its kind, was a huge bench that could cut strips of copper in a uniform size.

One day, Leonardo da Vinci found a strange lizard in the garden. He decided to have a little fun with the creature. He made wings for it from the skins of other lizards. He filled the wings with quicksilver, so that when the creature walked, the wings moved with it. He then made scary eyes, horns, and a beard for the lizard. He kept the lizard in a cage. When friends came to visit, he would pull out the creature, and the visitors would run away screaming.

Leonardo da Vinci also experimented with oils for painting and varnishing. He hoped to find a better way to preserve his art. On one occasion, Pope Leo asked Leonardo da Vinci to create a painting.

Leonardo immediately began mixing oils and herbs for the final varnishing coat of the painting. "Alas!" the pope exclaimed. "He will never do anything, for he commences by thinking about the end before the beginning of work."[38]

Although Leonardo da Vinci continued his experiments, he found little encouragement in Rome. Michelangelo, one of Leonardo da Vinci's bitter rivals, had finished his inspiring painting on the ceiling of the Sistine Chapel. He was the favored artist of the Romans. Another young artist, Raphael, was also at the height of his popularity in Rome. At age 59, Leonardo da Vinci had no desire to compete with these younger artists. He felt old and neglected.

Troubles seemed to pop up around every corner. Leonardo da Vinci's health began to suffer. At his studio, a hired craftsman was neglecting his projects to work for other masters. When Leonardo da Vinci complained, the craftsman reported him to the pope. The pope ordered Leonardo da Vinci to stop the work at once.

In despair, Leonardo da Vinci decided to throw his efforts into another project. He had always been fascinated by water. He began making drawings and

notes for a huge painting of the Great Flood. He
wrote a graphic description of what he wanted the
painting to look like:

> The air was dark from the heavy rain which was
> falling slat-wise, bent by the crosscurrent of the
> winds . . . It was tinged by the color of the fire
> produced by the thunderbolts wherewith the
> clouds were rent and torn asunder, the flashes
> from which smote and tore open the vast waters
> of the flooded valleys . . . [T]here might be seen
> huddled together on the tops of many mountains
> . . . men and women who had fled there with
> their children. And the fields which were covered
> with water had their waves covered over . . .
> [with] boats, and various other kinds of rafts . . .
> upon which men and women with their children,
> massed together and uttering various cries . . .
> [for] the waters [rolling] over and over . . . bearing
> with them the bodies of the drowned.[39]

The sketches that went along with this description were full of heaving waves, twisting walls of
water, swirling whirlpools, and toppling mountains.
In one sheet, an old man sat on a rock, with his chin

resting on his walking staff. His deep-set, sad eyes peered out over the tempest. Many believe this was a sketch of Leonardo da Vinci, watching the images of the end of the world. It may have symbolized the last years of his life.

Leonardo da Vinci never painted the Great Flood. Around this time, however, he finished what was probably his last surviving painting, of John the Baptist. Unlike the work of other artists, his picture shows the subject young and handsome. Even though Leonardo da Vinci was a sad, aging artist, he had not lost his vision of youthful beauty.

A FINAL JOURNEY

In March 1516, Giuliano de' Medici died. With him, went any of Leonardo da Vinci's hopes for greatness in Rome. Before the end of the year, Leonardo da Vinci received an invitation from the new king, Francis I, to come to France. Leonardo da Vinci was happy to leave Rome. His mind traveled back to that day more than 30 years earlier, when he had left Florence for the first time. He had accepted an offer by Lorenzo de' Medici to work in Milan. Now he was leaving Lorenzo de' Medici's son—

In this painting of John the Baptist, Leonardo da Vinci shows his subject as a young, handsome man. This was probably Leonardo da Vinci's last surviving painting.

Pope Leo—who had done very little to help his career. "The Medici created and destroyed me," he wrote in his journal.[40]

King Francis I was a true ruler of the Renaissance. He was strong and fearless in politics, but he was also enchanted by literature and the arts. Many monarchs loved the glittery display, but King Francis saw beneath the surface and understood what the artists were trying to do. He gave Leonardo da Vinci the small manor house of Cloux, near the king's favorite chateau, at Amboise.

Leonardo da Vinci relaxed in the lush green valley of the Loire River. King Francis demanded nothing from the artist, other than his company. The two men sat and visited often. The king later commented, "No other man had been born who knew as much as Leonardo."[41] At Cloux, Leonardo da Vinci received 700 gold pieces a year and was not pressured to finish work. He must have felt great relief, after all his years of troubles with unfinished commissioned paintings.

King Francis assigned Leonardo da Vinci to some engineering projects that were close to his heart—canal building. The king wanted a canal joining the Loire River to the Cher River. Leonardo da Vinci also designed a walled town with a river running through it. Water wheels from the canal supplied fountains throughout the city. Leonardo da Vinci, however, did not take on any major efforts of creation. His right hand became afflicted with arthritis, almost paralyzing it completely.

After all his years of probing the universe for answers, Leonardo da Vinci was plagued with an inner question in the final years of his life. "Tell me if anything at all was done," he wrote.[42] Compared to other artists of his time, he had finished few paintings. His great horse had been destroyed, and his scientific research was known only to his close friends.

Leonardo da Vinci could not see the dramatic effect his work had on his time. He had introduced a new approach to art. His engineering ideas had opened doors to incredible possibilities. During these final years in France, Leonardo da Vinci made one more marvelous design for a pageant. King Francis took part in the entertainment and Leonardo da Vinci constructed a huge lion for the performance. The lion lunged at the king and raised its paws, as if it were about to attack him. The king raised a magical staff and struck the lion. Suddenly the lion's body opened up. A great bundle of lilies—the flower of France—popped out. The court cheered at Leonardo da Vinci's creation.

Over the following months, Leonardo da Vinci's health continued to fail. In the spring of 1519, he sent for the royal notary to take down his last will and testament. He willed all of his notebooks, instruments, and portraits to Francesco de' Melzi, a friend and Milanese noble.

Florentines described death as "entering the great sea." They believed death was like falling into a peaceful slumber that a person could gracefully enter. Leonardo da Vinci did not want to resign himself to death, nor did he think it was the body's natural end. "The soul desires to remain with its body," he wrote, "because without the physical instruments of that body it can do nothing and feel nothing."[43]

He did not last much longer. Seven days later, on May 2, 1519, Leonardo da Vinci died. He was 67 years old. His life was not followed by a grand funeral procession. Instead he was buried quietly in a church at Amboise. Hundreds of years later, during the French Revolution, the church was wrecked, and his burial place was torn up. A gardener collected all the fragments of his body and buried them in a single grave. Years later, a French poet, digging in that very spot, claimed to have found Leonardo da Vinci's skull and some of his bones. The remains were reburied in the little chapel of St. Hubert in Amboise.

No one knows for sure whether or not the grave that claims to hold Leonardo da Vinci really does, but his sketches and notebooks leave behind more of a legacy than a grave ever could. The Renaissance man soared years ahead of his time. Sadly, he was underappreciated during his lifetime. Today, however, his work stands out to many as a wonder of humankind.

Test Your Knowledge

1 Upon his death, who succeeded Pope Julius?
  a. Giovanni de' Medici
  b. Piero de Medici
  c. Giulio de' Medici
  d. Pope John Paul

2 Who was the favored artist of the Romans?
  a. Botticelli
  b. Leonardo da Vinci
  c. Michelangelo
  d. Andrea Pisano

3 What are Leonardo da Vinci's sketches of the great flood believed to symbolize?
  a. The end of the world
  b. The end of Leonardo da Vinci's life
  c. The beginning of a new era
  d. The cleansing of the human spirit

4 What was the subject of Leonardo da Vinci's last surviving painting?
  a. Mary
  b. Jesus Christ
  c. Mona Lisa
  d. John the Baptist

5 How did Florentines describe death?

   a. "Entering the great sea"

   b. "Entering the vast ocean"

   c. "Entering another dimension"

   d. "Opening a new door"

ANSWERS: 1. a; 2. c; 3. b; 4. d; 5. a

1452   Leonardo da Vinci is born on April 15, in Vinci, to Piero da Vinci and a woman named Caterina; his parents were never married.

c.1462   Young Leonardo becomes an apprentice to Andrea del Verrocchio, in Florence, around this time.

1472   Leonardo da Vinci becomes a member of the Compagnia di San Luca, the painters' guild of Florence.

1473   Leonardo da Vinci helps to paint an angel in Verrochio's *Baptism of Christ.*

1479   Leonardo da Vinci witnesses the execution of Bernardo di Bandio and draws an account of it in his notebook.

1452 Leonardo da Vinci is born on April 15; his parents were never married

1495 Leonardo da Vinci begins his *Last Supper*, in the convent of Santa Maria delle Grazie

1473 Leonardo da Vinci helps to paint an angel in Verrochio's *Baptism of Christ*

1450

c. 1462 Young Leonardo becomes an apprentice to Andrea del Verrocchio, in Florence

1481 Leonardo da Vinci receives a commission to paint *The Adoration of the Magi*; he never completes the painting

1482 Leonardo da Vinci moves from Florence to Milan to work for Ludovico Sforza

1481 Leonardo da Vinci receives a commission to paint the *Adoration of the Magi*; he never completes the painting.

1482 Leonardo da Vinci moves from Florence to Milan to work for Ludovico Sforza.

1483 Leonardo da Vinci receives a commission to paint *The Virgin of the Rocks.*

1488 Leonardo da Vinci's teacher, Andrea del Verrochio, dies.

1490 Leonardo da Vinci begins work on a bronze horse sculpture in honor of Ludovico Sforza's father, Francesco, "The Thug."

1503 Leonardo da Vinci begins *The Battle of Anghiari*; he tries to build a canal from the Arno River away from Pisa in order to defeat Pisa

1519 Leonardo da Vinci dies at Cloux on May 2, at the age of 67.

1504 On July 9, his father dies

c. 1515 Leonardo paints *John the Baptist*

1520

1505 Leonardo da Vinci attempts to build a flying machine and perhaps tests it; he begins sketches for the *Mona Lisa*, which he completes sometime later; he gives up on *The Battle of Anghiari*, when bad linseed oil ruins the paint

1513 Leonardo da Vinci moves to Rome, to the Vatican, where he studies the properties of mirrors

1493 Leonardo da Vinci finishes a full-scale model of his great horse in clay.

1495 Leonardo da Vinci begins his *Last Supper* in the convent of Santa Maria delle Grazie.

1499 Leonardo da Vinci moves into a vineyard home outside of Milan in spring; the French army conquers Milan; he leaves Milan in December.

1500 Leonardo da Vinci arrives in Florence; he is commissioned to paint *The Virgin and Child with Saint Anne*, but never completes the project.

1502 Leonardo da Vinci travels with a military unit for ten months inspecting fortifications; he then returns to Florence.

1503 Leonardo da Vinci begins *The Battle of Anghiari*; he tries to build a canal from the Arno River away from Pisa, in order to defeat Pisa.

1504 On July 9, his father dies.

1505 Leonardo da Vinci attempts to build a flying machine and perhaps tests it; he begins sketches for the *Mona Lisa*, which he completes sometime later; he gives up on *The Battle of Anghiari*, when bad linseed oil ruins the paint.

1506 Leonardo da Vinci is summoned to Milan by Charles d'Amboise, the French governor

1507 Leonardo da Vinci is appointed King Louis XII's royal painter and engineer; he travels back to Vinci to settle his father's estate.

1513 Leonardo da Vinci moves to Rome, to the Vatican, where he studies the properties of mirrors.

c. 1515   Leonardo da Vinci paints *John the Baptist* around this time.

1516   Leonardo da Vinci leaves Italy for France; he serves Francis I in his court in Amboise.

1519   Leonardo da Vinci dies at Cloux on May 2, at the age of 67.

CHAPTER 2
A Lonely Genius

1. Serge Bramly, *Leonardo: Discovering the Life of Leonardo da Vinci*. New York: Edward Burlingame Books, 1991, p. 37.

2. Ibid., p. 40.

3. Charles Nicholl, *Leonardo da Vinci: Flights of the Mind*. New York: Viking Penguin, 2004, p. 46.

CHAPTER 3
The Young Apprentice

4. Nicholl, *Leonardo da Vinci: Flights of the Mind*, pp. 104–106.

5. Bramly, *Leonardo: Discovering the Life of Leonardo da Vinci*, p. 69.

6. Nicholl, *Leonardo da Vinci: Flights of the Mind*, p. 79.

7. Ibid., p. 80.

8. Ibid.

CHAPTER 5
Leonardo da Vinci's Studio

9. Nicholl, *Leonardo da Vinci: Flights of the Mind*, p. 139.

10. Ibid., p. 140.

11. Ibid., p. 160.

12. Bramly, *Leonardo: Discovering the Life of Leonardo da Vinci*, p. 174.

13. Ibid., pp. 174–176.

14. Nicholl, *Leonardo da Vinci: Flights of the Mind*, p. 181.

CHAPTER 6
In Milan

15. Nicholl, *Leonardo da Vinci: Flights of the Mind*, p. 184.

16. Jay Williams, *Leonardo da Vinci*. New York: American Heritage Publishing Company, 1965, p. 54.

17. Ibid., pp. 55–56.

18. Ibid., p. 57.

CHAPTER 7
Going Home

19. Williams, *Leonardo da Vinci*, p. 63.

20. Ibid.

21. Ibid., p. 65.

22. Ibid., p. 101.

23. Nicholl, *Leonardo da Vinci: Flights of the Mind*, pp. 498.

24. Williams, *Leonardo da Vinci*, pp. 107–109

25. Ibid.

26. Ibid.

27. Ibid.

28. Ibid., p. 117.

29. Ibid.

30. Ibid., p. 71.

31. Ibid., p. 75.

32. Nicholl, *Leonardo da Vinci: Flights of the Mind,* pp. 392–393.

CHAPTER 8
Taking Flight

33. Williams, *Leonardo da Vinci,* p. 83.

34. Ibid.

35. Ibid., p. 91.

36. Ibid., p. 93.

37. Ibid., p. 99.

CHAPTER 9
Entering the Great Sea

38. Bramly, *Leonardo: Discovering the Life of Leonardo da Vinci,* p. 388.

39. Williams, *Leonardo da Vinci,* pp. 127–128.

40. Ibid., p. 131.

41. Ibid., pp. 135–136.

42. Ibid., p. 138.

43. Nicholl, *Leonardo da Vinci: Flights of the Mind,* p. 499.

Bramly, Serge. *Leonardo: The Artist and the Man.* New York: Penguin Books, 1994.

Calder, Ritchie. *Leonardo & The Age of the Eye.* New York: Simon and Schuster, 1970.

Cooper, Margaret. *The Inventions of Leonardo da Vinci.* New York: Macmillan, 1965.

Hahn, Emily. *Leonardo da Vinci.* New York: Random House, 1956.

McLanathan, Richard B.K. *Leonardo da Vinci.* New York: H.N. Abram, 1990.

Nicoll, Charles. *Leonardo da Vinci: Flights of the Mind.* New York: Penguin Group, 2004.

Nuland, Sherwin B. *Leonardo da Vinci.* New York: Viking, 2000.

Payne, Robert. *Leonardo.* Garden City, NY: Doubleday, 1978.

Philipson, Morris. *Leonardo da Vinci: Aspects of the Renaissance Genius.* New York: G. Braziller, 1966.

Vallentin, Antonina. *Leonardo da Vinci: The Tragic Pursuit of Perfection.* New York: The Viking Press, 1938.

Wallace, Robert. *The World of Leonardo, 1452–1519.* New York: Time, 1966.

Williams, Jay. *Leonardo da Vinci.* New York: American Heritage Publishing Company, 1965.

Zubov, Vasilii Pavlovich. *Leonardo da Vinci.* Cambridge, MA: Harvard University Press, 1968.

Books

O'Connor, Barbara. *Leonardo da Vinci: Renaissance Genius.* Minneapolis, MN.: Carolrhoda Books, 1999.

Reed, Jennifer. *Leonardo da Vinci: Genius of Arts and Science.* Berkeley Heights, NJ: Enslow, 2005.

Romei, Francesca. *Leonardo da Vinci: Artist, Inventor, and Scientist of the Renaissance.* New York: Peter Bedrick Books, 2000.

Vezzosi, Alessanro. *Leonardo da Vinci: The Mind of the Renaissance.* New York: H.N. Abrams, 1997.

Websites

Leonardo da Vinci (1452–1519)
http://www.ucmp.berkeley.edu/history/vinci.html

Leonardo da Vinci: Renaissance Man
http://www.mos.org/leonardo/bio.html

Leonardo da Vinci's *Last Supper*
http://ccat.sas.upenn.edu/~lbianco/project/home.html

Medieval SourceBook: Giorgio Vasari
Life of Leonardo da Vinci, 1550
http://www.fordham.edu/halsall/source/vasari1.html

Rachel A. Koestler-Grack has worked with nonfiction books as an editor and writer since 1999. She lives on a hobby farm near Glencoe, Minnesota. During her career, she has worked extensively on historical topics, including the colonial era, the Civil War era, the Great Depression, and the Civil Rights movement.